CW00505958

Dear Nicholas . . .

A Father's Letter to his Newly Ordained Son

— MICHAEL HENSHALL —

With a new Foreword by
Stephen Cottrell, Bishop of Chelmsford
and an extended epilogue by
Nicholas Henshall, Dean of Chelmsford

Sacristy Press
PO Box 612, Durham, DH1 9HT

www.sacristy.co.uk

First published in 1989 by Churchman Publishing
This revised edition published in 2019 by Sacristy Press, Durham

Bible extracts, unless otherwise stated, are from the *New
Revised Standard Version Bible: Anglicized Edition*, copyright
1989, 1995, Division of Christian Education of the National
Council of the Churches of Christ in the United States of
America. Used by permission. All rights reserved.

Every reasonable effort has been made to trace the copyright holders
of material reproduced in this book, but if any have been inadvertently
overlooked the publisher would be glad to hear from them.

Sacristy Limited, registered in England & Wales, number 7565667

British Library Cataloguing-in-Publication Data
A catalogue record for the book is available from the British Library

ISBN 978–1-78959–064–7

Contents

Author's Preface to the Original 1989 Edition

Dear Nicholas was not written with publication in mind. It was a rather personal offering from father to son on a very special occasion. I am grateful to my wife, Steve Henshall, for her encouragement and to Peter Smith of Churchman Publishing for his. David Sheppard, the Bishop of Liverpool, with whom I have worked closely over many years, is a most encouraging, supportive and helpful colleague and friend. My secretary, Mrs Cynthia Hinton, has not only typed the script but also offered her own support and encouragement. I also owe much to the clergy and laity of the Diocese of Liverpool who are the gracious recipients of my ministry.

Michael Henshall
Bishop of Warrington

Foreword to the Original 1989 Edition

Dear Nicholas comes from the pen of a bishop who knows the clergy of the Church of England with a shrewdness and understanding; and he knows himself the pressures on newly ordained clergy.

Michael Henshall is an Anglican to his fingertips, loving the Church in which he was cradled, and at the same time firmly committed to the ecumenical adventure. *Dear Nicholas* discloses the authentic person inside the cope and mitre of a most effective bishop. The demanding calling to vigorous self-sacrificial living, undergirded by disciplined prayer is typical of the close colleague I have valued deeply for more than thirteen years in the Diocese of Liverpool. His most frequently preached text is from Timothy about stirring into flame the gift of God. But he is aware of the dangers of perfectionism, as he writes to his son Nicholas at the start of his priestly journey. He shows the distinction between an effective and a busy priesthood. Holidays need to go into the diary first: next spiritual discipline; then work.

The letters on Loitering and Beholding take the young priest into a needy world, resisting the security of becoming a private chaplain to some particularly demanding group. Priesthood is about being there with people in their needs and their celebrations. It is about comforting the uncomfortable and discomforting the comfortable.

Right at the heart of these letters is that about Trembling—trembling on the anniversary of his consecration—insisting on the mystery and transcendence, when the pendulum in the church swings too far towards mateyness with God. It comes out when he writes of his hero, Michael Ramsey, and of St Cuthbert, saints of the north east of England, where Nicholas has gone to serve. But most strongly the model which comes through is one we find in the Gospels. All this book is Christ-centred.

Here is not a complete compendium of priestly advice, but personal letters, springing out of well-observed experience, full of hints and insights. A newly ordained deacon or priest, or indeed one in mid-life, would find here priorities to cling to.

David Sheppard
Bishop of Liverpool

Preface to the 2019 Edition

Michael Henshall wrote *Dear Nicholas* as a personal letter to me, his son, when I was ordained deacon in 1988: a long letter in a series of short chapters. And for the occasion he had it printed out on good quality paper and bound in a simple red cover. But a letter none the less, not intended for publication. Dad didn't much care about legacy or reputation, and regarded most books as vanity projects. It was mum—Steve—who finally got it published.

So why this new version? The original edition had its moment in the limelight. Here was straightforward advice about living priesthood. One bishop used to give a copy to all those he ordained. And down the years—indeed, most recently just a few weeks ago—I bump into people whose lives have been influenced by this short text.

And it is published now, because reading it today it speaks afresh, with a genuine contemporary resonance. The Church I have served as a priest for well over thirty years now is one that has recovered its confidence in the apostolic faith, in its orthodoxy, and in its mission. It has also learnt the hard way that it now inhabits a different place in the world.

Dear Nicholas was a book of its time but turns out to be a book of this time.

Nicholas Henshall
Dean of Chelmsford (and Michael's son)

Foreword to the 2019 Edition

I began reading this book thinking it would open an interesting window on how the Church of England saw ministry forty years ago. I expected much of it to feel dated. I finished the book reinvigorated and surprised: not only had it focused on a set of insights into ordained ministry that are timeless, I felt refreshed in my own calling. The book's beguiling simplicity, and the fact that it is an actual letter from a father to a much-loved son, and not a treatise on ministry that the author ever expected to be read more widely, gives it an immediacy and a freshness. We eavesdrop on their conversation. There are references to people and events we can't know about. But we are better for it. We are drawn into the orbit of their exchange and their love. It also makes the book distinctively different from most of the other more worthy offerings in this overcrowded genre of good advice for others. No wonder several bishops have, for years, been distributing pirate copies of this text to those they ordain.

Of course, there is the odd occasion when the book reveals its age. But on the whole, and especially in its insistence that ministry belongs to everyone, and the prescient comments about being enslaved to gadgets, the book is startlingly contemporary.

However, it is that word "refresh" which beats a steady and stimulating rhythm throughout. The son in question to whom the father writes is a new priest, and the father an experienced bishop, and he contends that it is the spiritual disciplines established in the beginning that replenish and direct the ministry of a lifetime. This is where the emphasis on the eternal comes from, and with it the refining fires of darkness that the author so obviously encountered on his journey. These save the book from belonging only to one moment in time. In other words, this is not a book that tries to be relevant. That is its beauty.

And the other great theme of the book is love. In fact, the book is a kind of love letter. It exudes a sensible, godly love of the Church; a persevering and costly love for its people; a deep and stretching love for Christ; and, running through every page, a father's love for his son.

I don't know whether Michael Henshall was able to demonstrate his love for Nicholas in other ways. I hope so. However, I am aware that many men of his generation were not always good this way. But this book overflows with affection and delight as the pattern of ministry, and the collective wisdom of a lifetime, is handed, lovingly, from one generation to another.

Nicholas himself adds three fascinating vignettes; not so much a reply to his dad, but evidence that he has listened carefully. Those disciplines which shaped and refreshed his dad's life are shaping his and bearing fruit.

He focuses on a particular text: John 20:21: "As the Father has sent me, so I send you." I offer another. It comes earlier in John's Gospel—Jesus says it to his friends on the night before he dies—but in many ways Jesus' later words of commission flow from these words of reassurance: "As the Father has loved me, so I have loved you" (John 15:9). In reading this book we enter into that flow of love from *the* Father to *the* Son and from *a* father to *a* son and from generation to generation. It is a joyful, compelling and insightful read.

Stephen Cottrell
Bishop of Chelmsford

Introduction

Dear Nicholas

It has been a long and interesting haul from Altrincham Preparatory School via Manchester Grammar School and Oxford to Blyth (with Greece, Rome and Ethiopia as creative interludes on the way). I wondered how I could best mark it, not least your transition from lay to ordained. After all, to enter holy orders is a weighty and daunting step. When God puts his finger on us in this way—Watch Out!

Mum has perspired successfully over the construction of a lovely stole. I could have sought for an appropriate gift among the refined bric-a-brac of those purveyors of fancy ecclesiastical gear. But I set my heart on something a bit different. I dare not call it wisdom, nor should I vainly term it pearls. I have in fact gone quarrying in my sermons and articles, particularly those concerned with ministry. I have reflected a bit on the inadequacies of my own pilgrimage with lessons abounding. I have tried to gain insights about ordained ministry from twelve years as a bishop. As you begin, and as I start to see the finishing post in the distance, I offer some reflections.

First and foremost, I thank God for calling me to be a priest. I thank God that he found me Mum as companion on the journey. I thank him for Christopher and for Caroline—and for you, Dear Nicholas, you who now share with me his gracious calling into this mysterious privilege of priesthood. If I could start all over again, I should try to be more thankful. It is my rule to say the General Thanksgiving every day. I regret how mechanical that has sometimes been. I regret the times that it has gone with the wind. There is always something to say thank-you for at the end of even the most miserable of days.

Mum and I know full well that it is God who has chosen you.

We hope that it is not arrogance or parental pride when we think we had just a tiny part in it. Vocation is not only a mystery. It is something that is renewed; something that develops. I think it important to rehearse regularly the very first beginnings of it. Whenever I chair a selection conference for ordination candidates, I deliberately ask every candidate "When did it first begin?"

I remember a former Bishop of Chester shouting at you in Altrincham Vicarage: "What are you going to be, lad?" You replied—a terrified ten-year-old—"Same as Dad." Then some years later Mum supplied you with a Bible passage from the Acts of the Apostles (was it Peter's sermon?) for a school exercise. It spoke to you of vocation and priesthood. Then there was that School

Conference at York. We both hope that the philosophy— *it is not what you have, but what you are*—nudged you a bit. But all vocation, however helpful or unhelpful human agents may prove, is from God, is of God, is for God. When I was a parish priest, I used to say to my curates, "I'll never let you off. But I'll never let you down." That's how I think of God in Christ. I think that vocation partakes of that sort of thinking.

I believe that it was Augustine who insisted that grace works on the texture of our humanity. Grace harmonizes all the different aspects of personality. The incarnation is grace working on us as we are. You know something of my arrogance and sharp rejoinders. Where would I have been without grace? I know something of your arrogance (usually well disciplined) and your procrastinations. The priest particularly must consciously expose the texture of his humanity to the grace of prayer, the grace of sacramental action, the grace of scriptural power.

My maternal grandfather, caught in a November Stockport fog with his wife, gave the horses their head. "They will get us home," asserted my grandmother. They turned in at the first public house—and the second, and the third, and the fourth, and the fifth—it became a family joke. But my grandfather was caught, his addiction to alcohol revealed. Your own maternal grandfather, with a brilliant mind not unlike yours, if you will suppress the pride, ruined a great judicial or parliamentary career, by his addiction. Dear Nicholas, it may have missed a generation or so, but beware. Grace is needed when the tots flow! The texture of our humanity has to be exposed to his transforming power.

Mum, who knew me well before the grace of orders got to work, will tell you about the miraculous changes wrought! I am very far indeed from that heroic sanctity of which the saints speak, but I see it in the middle distance. I know that the magnet of his grace is at work slowly adhering the pile of jumbled pins that are me to the service of his glory.

My special prayer for you, Dear Nicholas, in the years ahead will be that his amazing grace will work on your own splendid gifts of mind and spirit. Who knows where such a process will lead?

The exegesis may be faulty, but I always say to priests that first and foremost we are called *to be with him*. Spiritual joy is the joy of that sort of relationship with our Lord. It is a joy that no one takes away. It is a deep movement in the waters of the soul, untroubled by outward troubles, oddly increasing as troubles come! "As they go through the valley of Baca they make it a place of springs" (Psalm 84:6).

The first little essay in this short collection is all about keeping fresh. However inadequately expressed, do heed the theme. I deal too often with broken and burnt-out priests. I see too often priests like stagnant water who have lost their vision. I sometimes see—and it is a sad sight—worldly priests, culturally smothered by the values of today. You have chosen, or rather been chosen, to walk a tight-rope, or to change the metaphor, to be a eucalyptus tree in the swamps of modernity. You will need to keep your balance: above all you will need to keep fresh.

Let some lines from a hymn end this introduction.

> Fill every part of me with praise;
> Let all my being speak
> Of Thee and of Thy love, O Lord,
> Poor though I be, and weak.
>
> So shalt Thou, Lord, from me, e'en me,
> Receive the glory due;
> And so shall I begin on earth
> The song for ever new.
>
> So shall each fear, each fret, each care
> Be turned into a song,
> And every winding of the way
> The echo shall prolong;
>
> So shall no part of day or night
> From sacredness be free;
> But all my life, in every step
> Be fellowship with Thee.

Horatius Bonar (1808–1889)

CHAPTER 1

Will It Keep Fresh?

Words echo in the memory. You can't have lived in our household for twenty-six years, Dear Nicholas, without hearing that question. "Will it keep fresh?" Mum and I first heard it in the Star Inn in Bridlington. We were newly married. We were both launched in our first jobs. I was an assistant curate at Holy Trinity, Bridlington. She was an assistant mistress at Bridlington High School. Precious pennies took us out to a Boxing Day dinner.

A loud, shrill voice of the sort that incites our failures in charity, was addressing their table—indeed, all the tables in the Inn. The subject, I vaguely recall, was some method of storing a vegetable. An equally obnoxious companion advanced some other theory. "Will it keep fresh?" "Will it keep fresh?" "Will it keep fresh?" came the mounting and crushing crescendo.

It is such trivial happenings that give birth to family traditions. For over thirty years now "Will it keep fresh?" has echoed and re-echoed in our lives. It comes very vividly to mind on the eve of your ordination. It lies behind so many of my prayers for priests. How do you sustain and develop a ministry over long years? "Will it keep fresh?" That is a critical question. Kindly address it, Dear Nicholas.

I can promise you our prayers day by day in our chapel, wherever we may be. I can offer you some thought quarried in the hard school of experience. Keeping fresh is fundamental to an effective, as distinct from a busy, priesthood. You have heard me often draw a contrast between reacting and responding. The priest who keeps fresh "responds". The priest who is simply busy "reacts". When souls are at stake, "responding" rather than "reacting" matters a great deal.

Just as a car requires servicing so too does the priestly life. There is the major overhaul (annual retreat, for example, carefully booked). There is the regular service (spiritual direction and sacramental confession). There is the mini service (the daily check: keeping open the windows towards Jerusalem). The contrast between those two passages in Galatians 5 should be at the very heart of your ministry. Learning to walk according to the Spirit, and learning how to reject life according to human instinct is a great art in itself.

These days "renewal" has become a cliché word. But renewal—daily, weekly, monthly, yearly—is all about "keeping fresh", about "stirring" the grace that is already yours.

When I had been ordained some twenty-five years, I did some research on my sermons. Which text from the

Bible had I preached on most? There was a very clear winner. It was from 2 Timothy 1:6–7: "I remind you to rekindle the gift of God that is within you through the laying on of my hands; for God did not give us a spirit of cowardice, but rather a spirit of power and of love and of self-discipline." That is a text about renewal. It has to do with Keeping Fresh. If Timothy, who lived in the halcyon days of the Early Church, needed reminding so soon of the grace that was his, how much more do we, all these centuries later, need to be so reminded.

As the years pass warm, subtle, comfortable, compromising ruts creep cunningly into the armour of ministry. Such ruts are the wrecks of many a ministry.

Let me draw your attention to a particular variety of caterpillar and to a particular experiment conducted by an eminent naturalist. In some of the pine forests of the world, there is to be found a category of caterpillar known as the Processionary Caterpillar. It is so called because like the elephants in one of Stanley Holloway's famous monologues, it advances through life, or to be more precise, through the pine forests, hanging on to the tail of the one in front. Hence the aptness of the description—Processionary Caterpillars.

The eminent naturalist rounded up a gaggle, or a flock or a cluster (or whatever the collective noun is for an assembly of caterpillars). He then painstakingly placed them round the rim of a large plant pot where, after the exercise of immense patience, he persuaded the caterpillars to do exactly what they did in nature and to hang on to the tail of the one in front. Eventually the circle was complete. The rim of the plant pot presented the fascinating spectacle of Processionary Caterpillars going round and round and round. In fact, in the experiment they continued to go round and round and round for seven days and seven nights without ever stopping. Then sheer fatigue, starvation and possible boredom meant that they started to fall dead from the rim—and all this despite the fact that just adjacent to the rim of the plant pot the eminent naturalist had placed an ample supply of goodies beloved of caterpillars and water in abundance. A reasonable change of course, and it would have been life and not death, it would have been beautiful butterflies, not stiff creepy-crawlies at the foot of the plant pot. Processionary Caterpillars. Processionary parishes? Processionary priests? Processionary bishops? Processionary churches?

I am superficially amused by the story of my caterpillars, but in fact it is a terrifying story of blindness, stupidity, refusal to change course, of that outlook which says, "We have always done it this way, and despite the salvation offered by good rations in another direction, we prefer to choose death." It seems to me that part of our integrity is to challenge the Processionary Caterpillar thinking, and of course we can only do that effectively if we take steps to see that we don't become Processionary Caterpillars.

I took part recently in an important discussion with the fascinating title "The Shape of the Church in the

Twenty-first Century". I contributed my caterpillar story. Somebody from a remote fenland village said, "Our parish is like that." Another said, "Ours was like that, but we got a new vicar 'full of eyes within', and it all began to change." I was fascinated by the use of the words from Ezekiel applied to the priest, "full of eyes within". Wisdom. Discernment. Courage. Vision. Inner toughness. Those are the characteristics suggested by the expression.

Growing in faith certainly requires us to take seriously the caterpillar story. But let me put it another way. Some years ago, you will remember that Bishop Festo Kivengere from Uganda stayed in our home. One evening he was talking about Kampala. He said that where the tarmac road came to an end as the city gave way to the bush, somebody had erected a notice. It read simply "Stay in ruts for forty miles". For forty years? For a lifetime? Ruts—deep, comfortable, alluring ruts which hinder growth and inhibit potential. They are very, very attractive.

I once asked a group of priests to write down a list of "clerical sins". What had tripped them up most in the course of their priestly lives? What had hindered—ruts apart—the process of Keeping Fresh? The list was formidable. It was probably overdone. Over beating of the breast by those orientated to perfectionism can in itself become a grave sin! Three sins headed all the rest. Activism. Procrastination. Accidie. Beware, Dear Nicholas, of this trilogy of ills.

Activism

You have heard my sermons over the years. You know that my exposition of the Doctrine of Justification by Perspiration always raises a polite Anglican titter. Demented activism is the reaction of deeply insecure priests to the signs of the times. We certainly live in a new Dark Age. We have to keep very fresh indeed if we are to avoid dark reactions to such a threatening scene. Oddly enough silence overdone, deserts oversought, retreats overindulged can all become an unhealthy response to the activists' pressures at work. The blessed word "balance" provides a solution. I speak, I think, from a former workaholic period. I learned my lesson when I learned to write into my diary—"Holidays". "Spiritual discipline". "Work". If the order begins with work the other two fade away. Fix your holidays. Fix your spiritual framework. Then do your work around those two supportive pillars.

Procrastination

Your gifts, Dear Nicholas, are great. I think that you have probably received the best education the world can offer. Manchester Grammar School. Oxford. Cuddesdon. What more! But there is even in you, dear boy, an element of procrastination. The great Duke was fond of saying: "Do the business of the day in the day."

Most of us know the perils of putting off until tomorrow the things that ought to be done today. At the time I thought it was a bit banal when Michael Ramsey said in my Ordination Charge in 1956, "Always pay your bills on time. Always answer your letters on time." He, with his massive perceptions, was charging us, as I charge you now, to fight actively against procrastination.

When I had been a bishop for a year, I realized the sheer impossibility of the expectations and the magnitude of the workload. I asked a management consultant for help. He it was who insisted on the holidays; spiritual discipline; work sequence. He also instructed me in the Pareto principle. Faced with twenty daunting tasks, arrange them in order, then number them in order of difficulty. Tackle the first three or four. You will then rattle off the remainder. It works marvellously. I have a daily sheet on which the principle is put into action. It is one clear answer to procrastination.

Accidie

Your forays into monasticism will have brought you in theory at least into contact with accidie—"the sickness that destroys in the noontide". The cell on the other side of the valley always looks greener and fresher! Accidie is a debilitating spiritual sloth. Of all the clerical sins it heads the list and is often unrecognized.

It is particularly prone to attack priests in the middle years.

You have a long time to go before you enter that particular tunnel. But it is the disciplines that you establish *now* that will help you *then*.

You have heard me make weak jokes about the midlife. But it is for real. Sadly, I see the spark go out in too many priestly lives somewhere down the long corridor of those middle years. Spiritual wells run dry. Serious reading becomes non-existent. Prayer evaporates. Worship diminishes. Alcohol or sex or money present problems. Accidie becomes a terrible testing reality. Those who survive have fought the fight long before. They have worked hard at establishing patterns of spirituality that will endure.

In the manuals on spirituality accidie is usually listed under sloth. Harton in *The Elements of the Spiritual Life* called it "the real canker of the spiritual life". It is a sort of spiritual gloom, a kind of heaviness that kills prayers and makes us feel spiritually depressed.

The answer to accidie is ultimately rooted in how a young priest, Dear Nicholas, establishes a firm, realistic, tough, but practical spiritual framework *that will last*. You are a fan of St Benedict. "Idleness," he wrote, "is the enemy of the soul." Hard physical work, like brushing a yard, can be an immediate response to the onset of accidie. But it is a spiritual network as well as physical hard work that brings us through this particular dark time. Beware of the middle years. They are best negotiated by preparing now.

Activism. Procrastination. Accidie. An unholy trinity of clerical sins. They all need watching like the proverbial hawk. But we can find help in an unexpected quarter. There are those about, Dear Nicholas, who appear to abhor what are called management skills when applied to ordained ministry. One of my episcopal colleagues once berated me when I held forth on the subject. But I regard a negative attitude towards management skills as an inadequate view of the incarnation! It's too spiritual by far.

Of course, priests are not managers. But equally, of course, priests have to manage themselves, their parish. Why not learn positively from those who know a thing or two in this field?

At the very heart of all management is the management of time. At the very heart of all priestly ministry is the proper management of time. We all start equal. We all receive a God-given 168 hours of the same commodity every week. Stewardship is about the creative, responsible, God-centred use of all those hours. Such management can help in the pitched battles we need to fight against activism, procrastination and accidie.

You remember that after I had been a bishop for some five or six years, I was invited to go on a course designed to instruct me on how to be a bishop. It was a typical Anglican oddity. Nothing when you start: tell you about it later! However, at one point the course required me to keep a diary. Under a number of important headings every half hour of every day was accounted for. The subsequent analysis was extremely helpful. It helped me to establish effective priorities, to review them each year and to set new ones.

In our Church Leaders' Group on Merseyside, Bishop David Sheppard and I are teased about our diary management, but I notice again and again how it pays off. I notice how some of my colleagues who don't believe in this sort of thing actually struggle to find dates when it actually matters.

You might like to have the eight headings that I often use to review my own work.

1. Maintenance of services of worship
2. Pastoral care and concern
3. Theological and related study
4. Teaching of the faith
5. Development of the faithful
6. Maintenance and development of resources
7. Prophetic ministry to the structures of society
8. Church concerns beyond the local.

You are fortunate to be close to Shepherd's Law, deep in Cuthbert country. Your own vocation owes not a little to visits there over the years. Harold's holy hill (or some equivalent "Sahara") should become at least an annual rendezvous. But if possible, climb more often your "hill" of transfiguration. (Remember a certain Eucharist there one August 6th?) Linger there with its holy man. Breathe deeply the heady air of eternity! Then your ministry down in the valley of Blyth (or wherever God sends you) will be kept fresh and in balance. Such pilgrimages will help you to keep the mystery of God present to people.

CHAPTER   2

Gods –With a Small g

Your life's work, Dear Nicholas, is to be an icon of Christ. In a special vocation, tried and tested, you are to be a mirror of God in your generation.

It helps greatly to have seen our Lord at work in the lives of others. Mum and I rejoice that your first appointment is in Northumberland. You will find St Cuthbert very much alive. With that powerful Celtic sense of the presence of God, Cuthbert was (and is) a mirror of Christ to his generation, but also to the generations that have followed.

I was recently called upon to name a church in Liverpool. There was fierce discussion. Some wanted this name, others wanted another. In the end I called off consultation. With due episcopal aplomb I chose St Cuthbert. There was immediate and widespread approval. All these centuries later his name evoked a response. He was truly an icon of Christ. His sanctuary in Durham Cathedral (the greatest building in the world?) is a place of pilgrimage. Spend time there. Wander in wonder its massive aisles. Call to mind another "saint" whom we knew and loved. To Mum and me Michael Ramsey was a "hero", a "god" with a small g, our very special icon of Christ.

It is a lovely memory that you met him in Oxford just before he died. His message to us through you came like pure gold. You were very privileged to see him "lying in state". What a memory to take with you through the ministry ahead.

It was at a very significant moment in my life that I met this large, wobbly, lovable man who was a mirror of the eternal God, who reflected with a clarity I'd never before experienced what Hans Küng has called "the dangerous liberating memory of the real Christ".

I first saw him on an October day of unusual splendour in 1949. His trousers were worn half-mast, his front was stained by many a breakfast and his ripped gown flowed in the wind like his even-then whitening hair.

I was an uncertain undergraduate, fresh from three years of army service, and oscillating between a career on the boards, at the bar, or in the ordained ministry of the Church. Let no one pretend that those years are easy. They are often days of doubt and despair covered up by the bravado of beer or the cultivation of some stupid eccentricity—odd socks or Siamese cats on leads. I think that I was slowly opting for the boards—those were the halcyon days of Wolfit's Lear and Olivier's Hamlet—when there was this man oozing holiness and reflecting in every sermon, every lecture, every informal talk "the dangerous liberating memory of the real Christ"; unconsciously weaving in the very being of a wayward undergraduate the stability and fascination of Jesus Christ.

We became friends—the friendship of the disciple for a master, the friendship of a student for a teacher and eventually the friendship that a man will always have with the bishop who makes him deacon and who ordains him priest. Over the years that friendship has endured, and it was a great moment for me in Liverpool Cathedral in our centenary year to stand alongside my great hero during one of the services.

I plan to outline five aspects of Michael Ramsey's character and abilities which over the years have reflected to me and many others "the dangerous liberating memory of the real Christ". These are not intended merely to inform you or even to entertain you, but to challenge you to discover in them as I have discovered something of that reflection of the Pattern Life—for ultimately Christianity is to be defined as being composed of those for whom Jesus Christ is ultimately decisive.

First, Michael Ramsey was one of nature's *priests*.

There are many debates and discussions today about the essential meaning of priesthood. When the responsibility of every baptized Christian for ministry is rightly stressed it becomes harder to define the particular responsibility of the ordained. *Why Priests?* asked Hans Küng in that powerful and radical little book. *To Maintain the Church in Apostolicity* defined Schillebeeckx in another important book on ministry.

Great music and great art, it is often claimed, communicate before they are understood and certainly great chords began to sound in my life when I met a man who so obviously stood on the God-ward side of human beings as well as on the human side of God—perhaps not a bad definition of priesthood.

In order to fulfil its mission, the Church needs persons who are publicly and continually responsible for pointing to its fundamental dependence on Jesus Christ. Among my cherished memories is the picture of Michael Ramsey delivering his ordination charge to those of us to be ordained on the morrow. I can't remember too much of what he actually said, but how he said it and the utter devotion to our Lord that was communicated has remained with me through the years. He radiated a sort of transcendence. You couldn't be long in his presence without being made aware of that great priestly word—holiness. It is clear that St Cuthbert had the same sort of impact.

Second—a great PR man. I don't use PR with its usual meaning of "Public Relations". Michael Ramsey was not particularly good at those—the sing-song voice, the great eyebrows, and the "er, er, ers" sometimes came over on the media as the caricature of an archbishop. I use PR to stand for something very, very different; for something that lies at the very centre of the Christian message—something that summarizes so much in

Michael Ramsey's teaching, preaching, writing and being; something which runs as a scarlet thread on the white snow of his reflecting message; something that you and I must grasp if we are to be faithful in our following of our Lord Jesus Christ. Passion/resurrection—dying in order to live.

The great redemptive work of Christ is not just something to be studied or acknowledged by the mind. It is something to be lived. It is the ground of our hope. The pattern of death and resurrection is to be the pattern of our lives.

Third—you can't talk about Michael Ramsey without talking about the great cause of Christian Unity. The Ecumenical Movement in this century owes him much.

I was within ten yards of Michael Ramsey in the chamber of the Church of England's General Synod when the vote rejecting the Anglican/Methodist Unity Scheme was announced. His whole posture—standing slightly hunched, with a drawn and puzzled face—showed the spiritual distress of hopes dashed and good ambitions frustrated. He was at that very fraught and vulnerable moment drawing on all those vast spiritual, priestly, biblical resources that made him a mirror of Christ—not just to me, but to many in my generation. Some insensitive victors in the Public Gallery applauded. The response from the archbishop was expressive of so much: "I think that silence would be the appropriate response", and the clapping collapsed.

He had spoken so eloquently and argued so passionately for that Scheme that I suspect its rejection marked the nadir of his tenure of the See of Canterbury and possibly the nadir of his entire pilgrimage. His contribution to the Ecumenical Movement has been massive, and he has been deeply trusted by many different churches and their people.

His sermons and addresses on Christian Unity tell of that commitment to the person of Christ and that regard for *his* Church from which we all can learn. And he never lost hope—the positive hope, hope against all the odds.

Fourth—it is, always has been and always will be a basic Christian duty to serve one's fellow human beings in a costly and demanding way; to take the towel and to wash the feet, and so to be a mirror of the master, a deacon of the faith. Service, it has been said, is the rent we pay for our room on earth—in Christ the service of God and the service of the least of the brethren are one. Service isn't something we can leave to some other Christian—it's part of the faith of Jesus.

Michael Ramsey served thousands and thousands by passing on to them, through a whole series of books and articles, great Christian truths that had come to him through costly study, prayer and reflection. His great love for Christ and for his body—the Church— his concern for disciplined prayer and worship, his emphasis on the wholeness and unity of life, echo and re-echo in his writings. They, just as the man himself, reflect Christ, mirror to us something of the life of God himself. Distilled wisdom, intellectual devotional insights, great sermons from great occasions—all are available in print and mark a major contribution of service to the community of God's people.

Fifth—the last, but certainly not the least of those Christ-like qualities I see reflected in Michael Ramsey, and from which we can all learn significant lessons, is simply his *humanity*. Christian maturity is never a matter of pulling ourselves together and being very impressive characters who have got it all right, who know exactly what it means to be a Christian and who have the willpower and the staying power actually to live up to it. It takes some of us a very long time to disown invincibility, and to acknowledge human weakness and vulnerability.

We serve a human master who went hungry and who wept and who rejoiced—not a stoic philosopher with a stiff upper lip—and in Michael Ramsey we lesser people saw vulnerability and humility and weakness and suffering and pain—but as we looked, we saw also the man of sorrows acquainted with grief and stricken. Michael Ramsey felt the battering force of the twentieth century as his master felt the battering force of the first century.

He could in his humility make you feel yes, sometimes lost for conversation; yes, sometimes embarrassed by the stuttering voice and twitching eyebrows—but yes, sometimes ten feet tall.

I remember as a very young member of the General Synod being asked with Mum to a supper at Lambeth. It turned out to be one of those nights when London traffic halted. We were late—very, very late. "Michael's dying to see you," said Mrs Ramsey, and he left his glittering guests, took your Mum by the hand, who he had not seen for several years, and said, "And how are your three children?" A prodigious memory. A very human archbishop.

I suspect for you that it may be Rowan Williams who will live on in your mind and inspire you from time to time. But as you get to know the north east of England, remember Cuthbert and Michael Ramsey—they were (and are) what Mum and I pray you are (and will be): a great icon of Christ to your generation.

CHAPTER 3

Pray Without Ceasing

Sermons can be dynamite. Preach well, Dear Nicholas. Spend time in "remote" and in "immediate" preparation. Make sure you are heard. Accept criticism. Ultimately as you well know, preaching, which isn't lecturing but proclamation, is all about communicating the mystery of Christ, the glory of God.

The principal of my theological college had a delightful, if pointed practice. As ordination approached, he presented a carefully chosen book to each of his students. His selections of titles were clearly not made from random. The very worst indignity was to be given a copy of Holy Scripture. At that late stage of one's training such a gift was seen as a massive rebuke, a judgement that one had seriously neglected the very foundation document of the faith. To be given a copy of William Law's *Serious Call To A Devout And Holy Life* also had an uncomfortable critical tilt in it. A secular book like *The Wind in the Willows* or *Three Men in a Boat* was seen as a hidden judgement that one was either unpleasantly pious or over-holy, or narrow and humourless. I recall a colleague being given a dictionary, and another receiving a volume of a work by Robert Louis Stevenson in which the word "donkey" was prominent, and yet another who received a fairly substantial volume dealing with problems of personal hygiene! The small volume that came my way has, as you know, been on my prayer desk for some thirty-one years, often read, always there as a reminder of the careful calculation that lay behind the selection.

I should say that in addition to the book the learned principal also wrote on the flyleaf in the Greek tongue a comment or quotation designed to offer a succinct view of some aspect of one's character.

The volume presented to me all those years ago was, as you know, by a certain Brother Lawrence, a cook in the kitchen of a monastery who wrote a spiritual classic, pointing to one of the essentials in all kinds of ministry. Technically the Prayer of Recollection is what he was talking about, but it's probably far better expressed by the title, *The Practice of the Presence of God*. I deduced from the gift that I was worldly, unspiritual, unholy, activist, lacking that basic sense of spiritual awareness so essential in any form of Christian ministry. In those now distant, but highly impressionable days the gift had quite a lasting effect. I concluded that I had been pointed in a very important direction. Better take note. Better attend to the deficiency indicated.

I did two things. One easy. The other difficult. I placed the book on my prayer desk where it has lived ever since, in order to remind me of the vital importance of trying to live the whole of my ministry in the nearer presence of God. Second, and more difficult, at least to start with, I began to get up very early in the morning. In fact, to do as Abraham did: "Abraham went early in the morning to the place where he had stood before the Lord" (Genesis 19:27). Not only was this a good precedent, there was another and a greater. Is it not recorded of the Lord of all life that he rose a great while before daybreak? Is it not said of him that he went to a desert place alone? Did not his closest followers come to the scene of the new creation with the stone rolled away—early in the morning? Over the long years I have come to value this Nazareth before the ministry, this quiet early morning start, this commitment to the beginning of each new day—to dwell, however imperfectly, in the presence of God, and in theory at least, to make it *the* priority in ministry. Time was when I was pretty strident about it: regarded it as a sort of eleventh commandment, and even imposed it on others. I have mellowed with the years, and while still deeply committed to what I like to call the ministry of the early morning, I recognize that what matters is not what time one rises, but what time one gives to God whatever time one rises. I simply note that those who leave it late often leave it altogether.

Our whole western society has been hijacked by the idea of achievement. That powerful philosophy inevitably, if not always consciously, spills over into the life of the Church and affects its ministry. In some church circles waiting in the dawn on the presence of God, investing time so that all time is redeemed, is seen as time lost to the provision of a soup kitchen, or is regarded as energy wasted in unhealthy escapism and piety, in navel gazing of an unnecessary kind. Yet more and more of all the essential priorities in ministry this seems to me to take priority over all else.

I preached my first sermon as a deacon to that text from 1 Thessalonians 5:17: "Pray without ceasing". It was, I suspect, a pretty indifferent offering. But it reminded me then, as it does still, that the prime priestly task is to communicate something of the presence of God. May your ministry, Dear Nicholas, be all about that basic spiritual work.

CHAPTER   4

Trembling

I have about half a dozen very clear memories of trembling. They all have to do with God, the only, proper person before whom a human being should ever tremble. Sadly, we live in a time of great casualness when trembling before God may well be regarded as suspect, even as unhealthy or described in terms of grovelling. I hope, Dear Nicholas, that your ministry will be full of trembling.

I have a clear memory of trembling before my Confirmation at the age of thirteen. I was surprised and a bit alarmed by the experience. I hid it away from the other candidates who seemed to me to be very blasé and untrembling—lest they should think that I was a cissy, or something odd. Sometimes now, as a person on the other end of confirmations, as it were, I occasionally notice the occasional candidate trembling, and I'm reminded of my own experience, for tremble I did and it was all very real and powerful—and it undoubtedly had to do with God.

On the day of my ordination I trembled in a bus all the way from the retreat house at Wydale to York Minster, a journey of some twenty-five miles or so. The night before I had seriously considered bolting, literally running for it, from those strong feet that had been after me for years, and here I was, cornered at last. I trembled like nobody's business on the morning when I first celebrated Holy Communion. It was in fact a near disaster as chalice and ciborium almost went for six. But again, it had to do with God.

Oddly enough, I didn't tremble on the day I was consecrated bishop, but I was very aware that the consecrating archbishop was shaking like a leaf. I have, however, trembled a bit on the anniversaries of my consecration—anniversaries are very important occasions, and ought to be kept—and I try always to keep mine as a very special day. It's then that I've found life a little uncomfortable by the onset of a bit of trembling. Again, it has to do with God. Or at least with being overawed by the realization of what it actually means to be called by Christ to a distinctive ministry within the Church. Trembling is a basic ingredient of any sort of ministry. It has been well said that the effective prophet is a mystic in action.

I know full well that my image back home wouldn't immediately be associated with trembling, but in fact I wish I trembled more, because both scripturally and spiritually trembling is significant.

Mark's Gospel is full of it—trembling, I mean. It's particularly prominent when the women arrive at the tomb on the morning of the resurrection, so prominent in fact that most scholars think that the true ending of the Gospel is at the words in Mark 16:8—"they were afraid". People see that as a sort of motif, a kind of theme indicating a basic attitude. Here is the great spiritual climax to the breathless story of the saviour of the world breaking into history. Human beings overwhelmed with the mystery and perplexity and bewilderment and transcendence of it all and being *overcome* with fear— holy fear—and trembling.

The whole Gospel of Mark is peppered with expressions indicating fear and amazement in the presence of spiritual reality—"they were amazed", "they became sore afraid", and at the end of the great story, with its rugged grandeur and mystery, with the empty tomb in focus and with a slow dawning of what has actually happened, they took to their heels in fear; trembling and amazement possessed their very souls. Silence and holy fear, awareness, awe, a sense of the numinous: all have their own messages. They tell, more than any words can, of the overwhelming reality of the resurrection, and I want to remind you—Dear Nicholas—that silence, fear, awe, mystery, amazement, trembling have a vital part to play in the prayer life of the Christian priest, as indeed in the life of every Christian. Spiritual poverty is being without that significant dimension. Trembling, in fact, isn't a sort of optional extra. It lies at the heart of everyone's response to the grandeur of the gospel.

We've become rather matey and huggy and pally in the Church of England in recent years. Just to give a personal illustration, in the past week during divine services I've been hugged three times, kissed twice and on one occasion embraced and well-nigh smothered by an entire charismatic congregation. I found myself wondering, after the smothering bit, just what Archbishop Fisher would have made of it all, and whether George Herbert, that great priest, poet and pastor, would have approved. Now, I'm not complaining about any of this. We somewhat stuffy, rather pompous and proper Anglicans needed to unfasten our safety belts, to thaw out and to understand afresh something positive about Christian joy and the meaning of fellowship, and in particular something of the meaning of celebration. But in order to make points, pendulums sometimes swing too far. Those of us who fought battles for the inclusion of the Peace in the Church of England liturgy didn't in fact legislate for "holy chaos", as it has been called, certainly not for ten minutes of trivial chit-chat and back slapping, but for a warm expression of corporate solidarity, liturgically expressed by a simple greeting.

The pendulum is in danger of swinging too far. The sinister side of the onset of mateyness is, in fact, the virtual disappearance of trembling. Once mystery and otherness and transcendence go out of the window, shallowness, superficiality and icing sugar come trotting into the ring. The skill is to have your cake and to eat it, to have genuine joy and fellowship welling up from an apprehension of the mysteriousness and otherness of God. Unless the two are held in balance, then there are very real dangers.

There are good reasons why priests in particular should be transcendent people—at least occasionally trembling before the King of Kings, who has extended to us such a gigantic privilege. However busy our parish is, if we fail to make prayer a priority then we are probably lost. The word transcendence means "climbing across", "going beyond", "exceeding the limits". It's a very dynamic word. Transcendent people are always on the move and are always widening their horizons. They are for ever unfastening their safety belts and avoiding those comfortable ruts and predictable patterns which beset us so easily. For transcendent people horizons are never impassable barriers—in fact, for the transcendent Christian there are horizons after horizons. Transcendence leads to deeper involvement in the world around, to a deepening, enhancing and enriching life. Transcendence lies at the very heart of ministry and it reminds us that the first priority in the priestly life is to stay in touch, close touch, with the transcendent life of Jesus Christ.

A tremble a day keeps the devil away. That may be crude, but it is an exact way of expressing the point. A deep commitment to prayer and to the prayerful study of the eternal truths revealed in the mysterious Christ lies at the heart of what ordained ministry is all about. The possibilities are immense. The apostle Paul put his finger on it when he said: "seeing the glory of the Lord . . . [we] are being transformed into the same image from one degree of glory to another" (2 Corinthians 3:18). We do have to provide space in our lives, real space, for seeing the glory of the Lord. That's where the trembling happens.

Paul clearly hints at an ascending progression towards God, to where we become, in Peter's words, "participants in the divine nature". Without transcendence, without trembling the priest, like any other Christian, becomes worldly in the negative sense of that term. The priest gets stuck within a limited horizon, then everything begins to go to pieces. When one Archbishop of Canterbury said, "I can never think of Almighty God as my pal", some folk were shocked, but others saw the point. "Pal" is hardly the word to apply to the cosmic, mysterious, transcendent Christ redeeming the world. The archbishop was making, much more effectively than I am, a plea for the mystery at the heart of Christian faith, a plea for avoiding trivial heartiness, a plea if you like for trembling, a plea for sustained prayer and meditation and for deep spirituality to be at the heart of activity— to underpin all activity, in fact, by the spirituality that arises out of waiting upon the Lord. We need to be able to say constantly with Jacob, when he dreamt on that great journey between Beer-sheba and Haran, "Surely the Lord is in this place—and I did not know it!"

Let the beginning and the continuing of your ministry, Dear Nicholas, be rooted and grounded in waiting upon the Lord: in the priority of prayer and worship, in the establishment of loving and developing relationships that arise out of a deep commitment to the transcendent Christ.

Let me suggest that there is a hymn which might well form the theme song, as it were, for this ministry. In my judgement, it is one of the greatest hymns ever written. It belongs in origin to the Eastern Church, where there is so much understanding of trembling and transcendence, and awe, and the numinous, in the living out of the Christian life. You know it well. Let it become a kind of theme at the heart of your ministry.

> Let all mortal flesh keep silence
> And with fear and trembling stand;
> Ponder nothing earthly-minded,
> For with blessing in His hand
> Christ our God to earth descendeth
> Our full homage to demand.
>
> King of kings, yet born of Mary,
> As of old on earth he stood,
> Lord of lords, in human vesture
> In the Body and the Blood,
> He will give to all the faithful
> His own Self for heavenly Food.

Rank on rank the host of heaven
Spreads its vanguard on the way,
As the Light of Light descendeth
From the realms of endless day,
That the powers of hell may vanish
As the darkness clears away.

At His feet the six-winged seraphs,
Cherubim with sleepless eye,
Veil their faces to the Presence,
As with ceaseless voice they cry.
Alleluia, Alleluia,
Alleluia, Lord most high.

From the Liturgy of St James, tr.
G. Moultrie (1829–1885)

CHAPTER 5

Loitering

Loitering with intent is a crime in English law. As one of the major priorities in the job description of a priest it is, Dear Nicholas, a virtue and moreover something of an art form. Long ago as a vicar, I learned personally the value of loitering with intent. I taught my assistant curates to loiter too. I suppose on reflection it must have been a pretty odd sight—a group of clerical gents of a wide age range, setting out after praying together to loiter in the streets of the town with deliberate intent. You recall our days at Altrincham. Loitering was part of our work.

I had to give it up when they made me a bishop—loitering, I mean. Bishops are in enough trouble as it is for daring to talk about the undesirability of selfishness in all kinds of high places, and for standing four-square for those at the bottom of piles. The press would have a field day if members of the episcopate took to loitering!

When I look back on the twelve years we spent ministering in Altrincham—not all of it spent loitering—I

can testify to the success of effective loitering. There
are, of course, some necessary preliminaries. It was no
use donning a pair of with-it jeans and a dirty shirt.
Effective loitering meant a clean clerical collar, and a
reasonably respectable appearance. It called too for
gospel confidence, because misunderstandings easily
arose. I recall a very naive and new assistant curate
being asked by a representative of the law what he was
doing hanging about in a seedy street. "Oh," he said, "the
Vicar has told me to loiter with intent." The situation
was amazingly complicated because on his way to his
loitering pitch he'd actually purchased a hammer and
chisel for some DIY task when he got home. It all took
some explaining!

Of course, a priest's job is about other activities as
well as loitering. It is about loving and challenging and
pastoring people of all ages and of all descriptions.
It is about avoiding the temptation and the security
of becoming a private chaplain to some particularly
demanding group or person. It is very rightly in these
days about ecumenical partnership and the effort of
will which that often requires. It is about preaching and
teaching the faith in all sorts of different and interesting
ways to sceptical and impressionable parishioners. It
is about helping the pretentious and the insecure to
take off protective masks, to discover themselves and
to begin their own pilgrimages. It is about comforting
the uncomfortable and discomforting the comfortable.
It's often about challenging expectations—not just

conforming to people's ideas of what a priest should be. It's about recognizing that there is a prophetic role as well as a pastoral role—the latter comfortable and affirming, the former demanding and often making for unpopularity. But to come back to loitering. In somewhat grandiose language I used to say to my curates: "You loiter as a sign of transcendence. You loiter as a symbol of unselfishness in a selfish world. You loiter in order to be available to crying need and to curious enquiry. You loiter to keep alive the rumour of God in an increasingly godless society."

There are a whole variety of reasons why I stress this theme of loitering. First and foremost, it is because we are very bad at it. Most of us, in fact, practise the opposite—that is, dashing headlong hither and thither in a state of hurry and perspiration. "Are you threatened by an empty diary?" I was once asked. I denied it vehemently like some unredeemed Peter in a courtyard, but I later admitted to myself that perhaps I was threatened. The great priest who for many years ran the now-closed theological college called Kelham, once wrote: "What you want of your parish priest is not primarily work. I wish the clergy would do ten times less and think ten times more. What you want of the priest is not just work but vision, sight and prayer." He was making an important point about spiritual loitering.

Another excellent reason for loitering in the street in the parish is that the exercise abounds in unexpected pastoral opportunities and contacts. Your grandfather was for many years the vicar of that small Cheshire village, Ashley. He used to loiter outside the village shop-cum-post office, especially on days when pensions or benefits were paid. He reaped a rich harvest from developing the skill of quiet contact and learning how to carry a conversation beyond the weather.

I can't even put a number on the calls that came my way as a vicar because of this loitering policy. For example, I remember loitering in a favourite street in the town of Altrincham. One afternoon a man rushed out into the road. He was at his wits' end over a major family problem. Some twelve months later the whole family—mother, father, three teenage children were prepared and presented for confirmation.

I like to think of our Lord in the Gospels as one who loitered. At the tender age of twelve, he loitered to some considerable effect in the temple at Jerusalem. Certainly he was master of the unexpected moment, of the unlimited opportunity presented by a sudden encounter at a well, or meeting a funeral procession outside a city, or being approached about the significance of a coin. Anyone who could speak of the ravens and of the lilies and of the grass in such spiritually evocative terms must himself often have loitered among them in the silence of creative prayer and reflection. In terms of pure excellence he was and is a sign of transcendence, a symbol of unselfishness and a marvellous responder to crying need and curious enquiry. His is the model for any of us, for any priest, for any Christian.

There are many definitions in today's church, many discussions, even arguments, about the job of the priest, the meaning of ministerial priesthood within a thankfully growing understanding of what it means to act upon and not just talk about the priesthood of all believers. There is general agreement that the priest is to be regarded as a representative person, who can't ignore the designation of leader; one who helps things to happen in the church and in the community and helps others to grasp the responsibilities implicit in their baptisms. But sometimes other language can be helpful. I chose the word "loiter" neither flippantly nor cynically, but with intent. Loitering helps to point up those three aspects noted in our Lord's earthly ministry. In a particular and special way, like the Master, the priest, Dear Nicholas, must be:

1. A sign of transcendence, sending out, in all that he does and says, signals of the wonder and the reality of God—keeping the rumour of God alive in the community to which he is assigned. I remember absolutely nothing of the words spoken by the priest who prepared me for confirmation as a thirteen-year-old schoolboy. I remember everything about the upright stillness of his praying body and the rustle of his cassock as he rose to instruct us. That man—who by his stillness undoubtedly had a share in my own vocation— must have loitered often with God in the quiet

of prayer in order to communicate something of the mystery of God to a thirteen-year-old adolescent. Learning more and more how to be a sign of transcendence in a world that has very largely forgotten what transcendence is, should surely be a part of our active ministry. He is, as you know Surtees Nicholson. He lives in retirement in Bamburgh. You might seek him out one day, Dear Nicholas.

2. A symbol of unselfishness. I don't think that it is just growing older that makes me say that selfishness, often subtle and crafty selfishness, is vastly on the increase in our society. Even in matters of spirituality there is, I believe, far too much gazing inward and far too little gazing outward at God, forgetting myself. It is possible for a parish to have a selfish outlook to other parishes, or a selfish outlook to the diocese or to the wider Church. It is possible for all of us to give way to intelligent self-interest and ignore the utter self-giving, the utter unselfishness of the crucified One. The selfish Christian is a contradiction in words, but without becoming a killjoy, or self-righteous, the way we keep Christmas, for example, is an illustration, just as the way we give is a barometer of our unselfishness, or the latter. In a whole history of detailed ways, the priest must strive, with their household, to be a symbol of unselfishness.

3. Responding to crying need and curious enquiry
    is basic serving and basic evangelism. A loitering
    ministry elicits curious enquiry. A loitering
    ministry is in a position to respond to curious
    enquiry. "Hey, mister; why are you hanging around
    my shop?" I was asked many, many years ago by
    an irate shopkeeper. "I don't like the things you
    are selling, particularly to young people," I replied.
    Years, literally years later, struggling to recognize
    his long-forgotten face, there he was in a group
    of confirmation candidates. We talked afterwards.
    That long-ago bit of loitering had undoubtedly
    been used by God. Touched a life, prompted a
    conscience. Space in a ministry, deliberately given
    to loitering, will be used by God, often in ways that
    will remain hidden from our eyes.

CHAPTER 6

Leadership

A group of priests, Dear Nicholas, were discussing the nature of their job. The first said, "I am a traditionalist. I tell my people what to do. I uphold the Creed and the *Book of Common Prayer*." The second said, "I regard myself as a stimulator of gifts, as one who enables lay people to be strong and effective Christians." The third said, "I see myself as a pastor, caring for people, loving people, serving people in joy and in sorrow." The fourth—a rugged-looking customer—said, "I always say to my people: 'Come on. Let's go.'"

Who was right? Which of the four priests would you choose to imitate? The traditionalist? The enabler? The pastor? Or the "Come on. Let's go" man?

Each definition contains an important truth. But, in fact, one of the four is much more significant than all the others added together. Which is it? I have no doubt, no possible doubt whatever. It is the rugged customer's definition—the "Come on. Let's go" priest. Why? Not just because it sounds like a person who acts or that the definition appears modern. No. But because in fact this priest is quoting our Lord, and set in context the quotation is totally significant.

Jesus said, "Rise, let us be on our way." He was in the Garden of Gethsemane. He was sweating out his vocation. He was tuning his human will to the will of the Heavenly Father. He was in agony. "Rise, let us be on our way." Where? Forward, to his Passion. Forward, to the cross.

The pattern of leadership in the Church, the essential model of ministry in the Church, the pattern of priesthood in the Church is that of the cross. "If any want to become my followers, let them deny themselves and take up their cross and follow me" (Matthew 16:24). We are constantly tempted to import the world's models of leadership into the Church. Jesus was clear-cut and unambiguous in his condemnation, "It will not be so among you" (Matthew 20:26). The chief pastors of the Church, whether they are bishops or whether they are priests, are to lead by carrying a cross, as Jesus did. That's why St Paul was so successful in ministry. At Corinth his authority was challenged; when he was, as it were, required to produce his credentials of leadership, he appealed solely and simply, but powerfully and effectively to the fact that he followed the way of the cross: "As servants of God we have commended ourselves in every way: through great endurance, in afflictions, hardships, calamities, beatings, imprisonments, riots, labours, sleepless nights, hunger . . . We are treated as impostors, and yet are true; as unknown and yet are well known; as dying, and see—we are alive; as punished, and yet not killed; as sorrowful, yet always rejoicing; as poor, yet making many rich; as having nothing, and yet possessing everything" (2 Corinthians 6:4–5, 8–10).

Come on. Let's go. "Rise, let us be on our way." And Jesus goes before them to the cross. Such is the pattern of leadership for the Church, and it overrides all other models and considerations. Every society needs the right kind of leadership in order to be effective. We know from our history that the wrong form of leadership in the Church or in the world can play havoc with and destroy communities. Those of us in holy orders, whether we are responsible for giving a lead in a diocese or for giving a lead in a parish, should think often and deeply about the pattern of our leadership, and before all the other considerations with their proper insights and validities, it is to the discipline and dedication of the cross that we must look. And whenever we fall down in our leadership, as fall down we certainly will from time to time, it is in the power of the cross that we pick ourselves up and resume the way.

In these days, when the applause often goes to the social gospeller or to the Christian activist, it has become ridiculously unfashionable to preach the cross. All Christians, but particularly those called to an office of leadership, must know without doubt that what is expected of them is to follow the way of the cross, which is basically a way of total unselfishness, a way of suffering, a way of pain, but an effective and positive way. "Come on," said our Lord, "let's go."

A great deal of present preaching and teaching often appears to sidestep the centrality and significance of the cross. Jesus is portrayed as simply offering a guarantee of peace, happiness and security for this life and for eternity. The tough, crucial elements are certainly far from prominent. They are muted and soft pedalled. "If any want to become my followers, let them deny themselves and take up their cross daily and follow me" (Luke 9:23).

Dietrich Bonhoeffer, killed by the Nazis, coined the interesting expression "cheap grace". Part at least of what he meant had to do with Christians ignoring, or sidestepping the outrageous, demanding challenge of the cross in personal and community terms and opting for a gospel of comfort and security.

In our own country, Christianity has been around for a very long time. It is easy, because of that, for it to lose its cutting edge. Easy for the hard, demanding bits of the gospel to be tuned down to suit our personal or social convenience. Easy to forget or to ignore the powerful challenge of the gospel to take our Lord and his message seriously. All of that process would fit under Bonhoeffer's expression "cheap grace".

Whenever and wherever the faith is relegated to the margins of life, whenever and wherever the faith is simply a sort of an appendage to an otherwise conventional life, there is "cheap grace" at work. Our

faltering eyes must turn constantly to the cross with its
message that unselfishness and discipline and courage
and perseverance matter. And any who opt for "cheap
grace" are challenged afresh by having their eyes
directed, however uncomfortably, to the crucified Lord
of glory.

Of course, with varying emphasis the points made by
that group of priests discussing the nature of their job
should not be lost.

Tradition is important. The trouble with tradition
in English society at the moment is that it is being
allowed to degenerate into nostalgia and nostalgia is
most decidedly not a Christian virtue. The danger, for
example, of sixteenth-century forms of worship is that
they convey sixteenth-century ways of thinking that
are quite out of tune with today. Tradition should be
carefully preserved lest it become debilitating nostalgia.

A pastor? Well, naturally. Obviously. Clearly.
Although it is not easy to be a really good pastor. Of
the Good Shepherd it is written that he calls the sheep by
name: that should be never far from our consideration.
At the same time, it is sometimes easy to opt for the role
of pastor and forget the uncomfortable role of being a
prophet.

But at the heart of the ministry of leadership,
illustrating and informing all the other aspects, is the
contribution made by the rugged-looking customer in
the discussion. "I always say to my people: 'Come on.
Let's go.'"; "Rise, let us be on our way." Let us be going to

the agony, and the glory, and the life that is to be found only at the foot of the cross—the daily, hourly source of all ministry, whether it is ordained or lay. You love, as I do, that verse from a great hymn:

> God is Love: and he enfoldeth
> all the world in one embrace;
> With unfailing grasp he holdeth
> every child of every race.
> And when human hearts are breaking
> under sorrow's iron rod,
> Then they find that selfsame aching
> deep within the heart of God.
>
> *Timothy Rees (1874–1939)*

(NB These are the words of the hymn as Timothy Rees actually wrote them and as it is normally sung, but there is a whole family of hymn books that find this so shocking they change the words of the second half of the verse!)

CHAPTER 7

Discipline

I recently read, and then re-read Richard Foster's *Celebration of Discipline*. I think, Dear Nicholas, we share an admiration for this great spiritual "classic". The subtitle of that important book is significant. It is called "The Path to Spiritual Growth". The opening sentences of the book are worth quoting in full:

> Superficiality is the curse of our age. The doctrine of instant satisfaction is a primary spiritual problem. The desperate need today is not for a greater number of intelligent people, or gifted people, but for deep people. The classical Disciplines of the spiritual life call us to move beyond surface living into the depths. They invite us to explore the inner caverns of the spiritual realm.[*]

---

[*] Richard Foster, *Celebration of Discipline (*Hodder & Stoughton, 1980), p. 1.

Ours is an age that tends foolishly to undervalue discipline.

We agree about the significance of daily prayer and of regular Bible study and of sustained worship and heroic service. We nod our heads in a sage manner about the importance of reaching out and of studying and of wrestling with the great issues of Christian belief. But ignorance remains the great debilitating factor, and those who carry out surveys report time and time again about the absence of prayer and reflection and meditation within the Christian life, while a significant discipline like fasting is almost non-existent in a greedy, consumer-orientated society.

In Christian spirituality, discipline usually needs to be self-imposed. It is to do with the will and the training of the will. Without discipline, ingrained habits take up their abode in us and important doors remain closed. Discipline is one major avenue to growing in faith, what T. S. Eliot calls in "The Dry Salvages", part of *The Four Quartets*, "an occupation for the saint".

Not many of us are saints, with the gifts that belong to that very special and unusual calling, but as the poet expresses it, yes, there are moments of insight, hints of glory, but "the rest is prayer, observance, discipline, thought and action".

There is one rather special area that calls out for observance and discipline. Little evidence exists to suggest that our theological colleges adequately prepare the unmarried for what on one level can be a lonely priestly life. After years in a university or college community suddenly—as you know—the ordained person can be living all alone cooking or not cooking, coping or not coping, cleaning or not cleaning! A very particular grace and a very special discipline must be sought by the single. Horrid temptations lurk not least in leisure. An over-dependence on alcohol is not unknown. Illicit sexual dabbling can overtake the unwary. Of course, discipline is for all; for all must tame Brother Ass. But an especial vigilance is needed today by the single. The seat of the conflict is always the will.

That is where all battles to do with discipline are fought. Meditate often on Jesus in the Garden of Gethsemane. That is a key passage for the training of the will whether we are single or married.

CHAPTER 8

Coping with Change

You may recall, Dear Nicholas, that a large crystal ball
sits on my study desk. It was given to me by David
Pilkington after an official visit to the famous glass works
at St Helens. I am fond of preaching on the well-known
text from Proverbs, "Where there is no vision the people
perish" (Proverbs 29:18). In search of inspiration, I often
pick up my crystal ball.

As your ordination approaches, I have found myself
wondering about the great issues that you will face as your
ministry unfolds. What is your vision? What issues will
matter most to your generation? Some will be new issues,
demanding new responses. Others will be a continuance
of issues with which my generation has had to grapple.

There looms ahead the horrendous problem of offering
pastoral support and an effective spirituality to AIDS
sufferers and their dependents. There is the complexity
of proclaiming the uniqueness of Christ in the midst of
a multi-faith world. There is (is it our last chance?) the
evangelical task of tapping into the shrinking, residual

Christian faith in our western society. There are all the
issues that gather round advances in technology, from
nuclear power to enslavement by gadget. There are
philosophical and theological issues to be faced against
the backcloth of a shop-soiled materialism and a deep-
seated determinism amounting to fatalism. There are
vast problems connected with the environment and
climate change, calling out for a Christian critique.

There is increasingly the ecumenical agenda. You know
that being a member of the Church Leaders' Group in
Liverpool and sharing in the Mersey Miracle has been one
of the great experiences of my life. I never worked harder
than when writing "Call to Partnership". It is a great,
personal delight to see all the recommendations of that
important working party actually coming into operation
in the Ecumenical Assembly and in the Departments of
that Assembly, here in Liverpool. In a city that for decades
was immersed in sectarian strife of the very worst kind,
I have seen with my own eyes the creative power of our
Lord's reconciling work. Such experiences speak to me of
the reality and power of the gospel. The Mersey Miracle
is the story of church communities growing in faith, but
I can also tell you that the spin-off in terms of personal
growth is highly significant. Ecumenical co-operation
is not just a fashionable exercise. It is a deep response to
Jesus' High Priestly prayer in John 17. It is costly, and it
is a significant way of growing in faith. In these days we
all need to commit ourselves as pilgrims to ecumenical
partnership as a means of growing in our ministry. I

hope very much that it will be a part of your pilgrimage and of your growth.

But you plug in, as it were, to a continuing agenda. Perhaps it is best described as freeing the Church from its medieval captivity. Large chunks of my ministry continue to be dominated by attempts to reinstate the laity as an active and full part of the ministry of the Church. It is a battle that remains to be won.

I think it was John Robinson who said: "The laity are not the helpers of the clergy so the clergy can do their job, but the clergy are the helpers of the laity so that the laity can be the Church in the world." God's Frozen People are only gradually becoming God's Lively People. There is a great prize still to be won. It is nothing less than the recovery of the New Testament concept of ministry. You will recall that lovely little cameo called *Opting Out*:

> There are 566 members in our church.
> But one hundred are frail and elderly.
>> That leaves 466 to do all the work.
> But eighty are young people at College.
>> That leaves 386 to do all the work.
> But 150 are tired when they come home from the
>> office. That leaves eighty-six to do all the work.
> But forty-six have most important outside
>> interests. That leaves forty to do all the work.
> But fifteen live too far away to come regularly.
>> So that leaves twenty-five to do all the work.

And twenty-three say that they've already
    done their bit for the church.
That leaves YOU and ME.
And I'm EXHAUSTED.
GOOD LUCK TO YOU!

You have heard your nonagenarian grandfather say that
he and the members of his generation have lived through
more change than any other generation in the history of
the world. One of my great priorities has been to attempt to
help Christian people to cope with change. Sadly, success
is a slow matter. Your ministry, at least initially, will be set
in the warm communities of the north east. You will find
that you need all your skills to help people cope creatively
with change. The exposition of the doctrine of creation
may well prove to be the key that unlocks the door. I like to
believe that there is a real sense in which we still live in the
sixth day of creation, co-operating with God in his process
of continuous creation. It may, for example, help us to
value people, not in terms of work but for what they are
in themselves, people created in the image of God. Issues
of unemployment remain, but now on the horizon there
is the problem of an ageing population. Your generation
may find itself very stretched in order to look after the
white hairs and ailing limbs of my generation!

    After my last period of study leave in 1982, I was asked
to write a paper for our Bishop's Council. I called it, you
will remember, *Seismic Upheavals*. It was an attempt to
analyse cataclysmic change. It was designed to help the

Diocese face realistically the many issues that gather round the word "change". You will recall heated discussions round our family table. There was creative conflict over expressions like, "We have come to the end of Renaissance Man [sic!]", or "the myth of the Enlightenment". But we all agreed that the philosophy of determinism has got our western world by the throat. We also agreed that the results of change—fast-paced technology; multi-faith issues; political and economic and social uncertainties—cause great problems for those to whom we minister.

I remember our amusement at the story of the chameleon brought back to Britain by an ardent explorer. He enjoyed taking it to parties. He placed it on people's clothing. It obligingly changed colour. One day he took it north of the border. He placed it on a tartan kilt. The poor creature became so confused that it lost its facility and became disorientated. That sort of chameleon-like confusion is fairly widespread in our parishes.

May I advise you, Dear Nicholas, to examine with care reactions to change among the flock entrusted to you. You will find, in fact, that people react rather than respond. Only by careful analysis will you be able to formulate an effective ministry. For example, the cult of nostalgia is heavily in evidence in many of our churches. Battles about the alleged beauty of the *Book of Common Prayer*, and the alleged banality of contemporary forms of worship are rarely informed liturgical battles. They are battles about change: about a preference for air-raid-shelter theology: about a failure to distinguish between nostalgia and tradition. A loving, but challenging, teaching ministry lies at the heart of helping the faithful not to get stuck in the ruts of nostalgia.

Then there is the cult of simplicity. People like their faith cut and dried. Above all they like it "definite". Many tilt at the Durham windmill, because it presents a threat to a simple faith. The seventeenth-century Church was nasty to Galileo. The nineteenth-century Church was nasty to Huxley and the scientists. Some of those same attitudes are being rerun in the twentieth-century Church. That is not to its credit.

You know by heart some of my favourite quotations. Remember one from Owen Chadwick's great book, *The Secularisation of the European Mind in the Nineteenth Century*: "Defenders of Christian orthodoxy looked to their gates, lowered the portcullis, raised the drawbridge and boiled the oil." Your ministry must help fearful Christians to find confidence to face the issues.

Use your intellectual gifts, Dear Nicholas, to help people prone to nostalgia and simplicity to handle paradox and to be undaunted by complexity. You will need the skill of a pilot: the patience of a fisher: the toil of a labourer: the knowledge of a guide: the courage of a prophet: the clarity of a teacher: the tenderness of a father: the care of a shepherd: the alertness of a watchman: the faithfulness of a steward: the address of an ambassador. That is a tall order, Dear Nicholas, but in *his* gracious and splendid *name*, "I can do all things through [Christ] who strengthens me" (Philippians 4:13).

CHAPTER 9

Beholding

There is, as you well know, Dear Nicholas, a great and continuing debate in our Church about the meaning of ministry. I hope that in the course of time you will make your own distinctive contribution to that debate. It can be helpful to light upon a single word which can serve to illuminate the debate. Sometimes it is the tiny little words in scripture, the apparently unimportant ones that actually open the windows and let in light and air. I therefore invite you, Dear Nicholas, to consider the little word "behold". It occurs often in scripture. On several occasions it features in the different accounts of our Lord's Passion.

On a Good Friday I have sometimes preached from the text from Lamentations, "Behold, and see if any sorrow be like my sorrow" (1:12). "Behold" is a stronger word than "look". It is a deeper word than "see". Behold is a call to pause and to penetrate deep into the mystery of something.

To doubting Thomas, our Lord said, "Behold my hands and my feet, that it is I"(Luke 24:39). That is a powerful command to look at his resurrection body and take to heart, "it is I". Pilate, twisted up with his Roman sense of justice and his own miserable self-interest, says, "Ecce Homo—behold the man", and then there are those words put into Jesus' mouth by St John in the last book in the Bible: "Behold, I stand at the door and knock" (Revelation 3:20).

But in the whole of scripture—no, in the whole of history—was the word ever more solemnly or significantly used when it was twice spoken from the depth of his agony, from the uplifted cross, "Woman, behold your son"; "Son, behold your mother" (John 19:26–27)? It is a supreme and superb example of pastoral ministry: of a caring, a concern, a compassion, a regard for the other without reference to his own suffering, and thirst and dereliction. How dare we ever not care when he cares so gloriously?

In the same way, it can be pastorally comforting to recall that later on in the unfolding drama of redemption, another little word echoed and re-echoed from the central cross—"Why". "Why have you forsaken me?" Those of us in public ministry can all recall the harrowing and perplexing questions from the bereaved or the dying. Why. Why. Why. It is immensely comforting to know that the saviour of the world used the same bewildered cry in his great agony on the cross.

Beholding belongs to the very essence of ministry. My prayer for you, Dear Nicholas, is that you will become a good beholder. We have talked from time to time about that great resurrection story—the race of Peter and John to the tomb. I know that your precise, classical scholarship may not, in fact, regard the three different words for "to see" as being of ultimate significance. But they are different words. They are translated in English by the word "to see". The first means casually noticing. The second means beginning to focus. The third means penny-dropping. True beholding comes into that third category. Seeing beyond the obvious: penny-dropping.

A black man told me that again and again he was treated as if he were just a black man, not a person with a name. "People don't behold me," he said with a marvellous insight. A woman using a wheelchair said, "The advert is true. People never see a person in a wheelchair. They see a wheelchair." She was really saying something very significant about the need to behold. Anyone who has had anything at all to do with marriage breakdown, or helping with matrimonial problems, knows full well that at some point the couple had ceased to behold each other.

Dear Nicholas, your ministry is very much a beholding experience. You must behold particularly those you don't like. You must behold in detail those within the Christian community. You must behold your vicar and your bishop. You must behold those who have proper authority over you, as well as those whom you serve. I sometimes hear members of the laity speaking of their priest in very impersonal terms. In one parish I heard them referring to "'im". "'Im" turned out to be the vicar. It was very poor-quality beholding.

There are many aspects of beholding that are of importance for the minister of the gospel. As leaders of the church we must behold the signs of the times, have some grasp of the forces at work in our society which contribute so much to our ministry. But most central of all is the discipline of beholding our Lord in every aspect of ministry. By such beholding, Dear Nicholas, we become icons of Christ.

CHAPTER 10

Anima Christi

There are, Dear Nicholas, some prayers that last for ever! The *Anima Christi*, older than the Ignatian Exercises that it heads, is to be numbered among them. You learned it by heart in the long-ago of the catechism class at Altrincham Parish Church. I tried as a parish priest to teach it to generations of confirmation candidates. I always invite the congregation at a Three Hours Devotion on a Good Friday to recite it between Meditations. We say it daily in chapel, as you well know, at the end of Matins. I use it too as a preparation and a thanksgiving when I celebrate the Eucharist. Over the years great chords begin to sound.

All of us should know by heart a handful of the great prayers. I recall an ex-catechism boy from my first parish of Micklehurst telling me that the *Anima Christi* had saved his life. He was shipwrecked in the Pacific. He simply recited the prayer until he was rescued. Use it often, Dear Nicholas. It will help you never to stray far from the tough and exhilarating walk with the Lord of all Life.

> Soul of Christ, sanctify me.
> Body of Christ, save me.
> Blood of Christ, refresh me.
> Water from the side of Christ, wash me.
> Passion of Christ, strengthen me.
> O good Jesu, hear me.
> Within Thy wounds hide me.
> Suffer me not to be separated from Thee.
> From the malicious enemy defend me.
> In the hour of my death call me,
> And bid me come to Thee,
> That with Thy Saints I may praise Thee,
> For ever and ever. Amen.

"As the Father has sent me, so I send you" (John 20:21)

A brief response to "Dear Nicholas . . . " by
Nicholas Henshall, three decades on

Here I don't really want to add much to what you wrote then (and which I promise I have only slightly revised!). But I do want to say something in the following short pieces. None of the stories or reflections here will be unfamiliar to you. They pick up themes that you and I have spoken of again and again over the years—themes that have formed, and I hope been visible in, our very different ministries as ordained elders. It is a bizarre coincidence that I am writing this just as I reach thirty-two years of full-time ordained ministry, exactly the length of your own ministry when you first wrote me this letter. You know that great line of Kierkegaard that the trouble with life is that we have to live it forwards but only understand it backwards! Maybe it's only at this point—where, as you say, you begin to glimpse the finishing post—that you really begin to see the shape of the journey you've been on with the Lord.

I offer no apology for the title of this section. OK, there is the danger of a typical Henshall play on words. But John 20 is probably the text I have preached on almost more than any other (the one I have preached on more often is Genesis 32, Jacob's night-time fight with God at Peniel, but that's for another time!).

Here at Chelmsford Cathedral the line "As the Father has sent me, so I send you" has become the foundation on which we've sought to establish the whole narrative of the cathedral's life. It's only ever going to be a work in progress. But I think both of us share that passionate conviction that the Church needs to rediscover that it is fundamentally a *sent* community. "Apostolic" to use the New Testament word. A community that goes where Jesus goes and does what Jesus does.

Love in action

Colin was murdered in his flat a few hundred yards away from the cathedral a few days short of his fortieth birthday. It had been a complicated life, and a tragic end. When I heard the news—like many people, I suspect—there was that deeply unpleasant frisson of excitement. A murder, here in Chelmsford! I even watched the local news for more information—not because I wanted to be informed but because of that awful desire to be involved vicariously, in the same way as the traffic slows on the motorway because of a car crash on the other side.

The following day, after Morning Prayer and the Eucharist a group of us were walking out of the cathedral to grab a coffee. We walked straight into the person who had found Colin's body. I was thinking about anything else but that—a presentation I was doing that afternoon; a difficult email I needed to write; where I was going to buy some wool that I needed for a discussion group (yes, really). I'd slept badly too. Soon we were all drinking coffee together and listening to a person in deep, deep shock.

I felt immediately stupid. This wasn't glamorous or exciting. This was the awful impact of violent death on other people—family, neighbours, friends. And then the discovery that, of course, Colin was not a stranger but part of the cathedral's extended family. Colin had been a regular at the Wednesday afternoon drop-in which serves some of the networks of vulnerable people in the city centre. Unsurprisingly, Colin had been barred on Wednesdays, because he refused to muzzle his Staffordshire Bull Terrier. But that's often how relationships in extended families work.

I felt deeply humbled. I had been filled up with the busyness of the day to come, tired from a bad night's sleep and a little excited (in a sick sort of way) by the news of the murder the day before. And here was reality—the reality of human need and of what a cathedral, what a church actually could be for other people. A place where people find comfort, refuge, sanctuary—not just in a building but through the networks of the people—because this ministry of service is known, valued and effective.

I don't want to misuse a tragic local event for my own rhetorical or theological ends. But I do want to suggest that it is a graphic illustration of the ministry to which the Church is called as the active ingredient in the life of the wider community which it is there to serve, with a gospel bias to the poor.

The mandate is clear enough. Jesus makes it absolutely clear that ministry to the marginalized, the broken and the lost is the first priority of the Christian community, not an added extra. It is the major theme of Jesus' first sermon in Luke 4:16–21 and his last piece of discipleship training in Matthew 25:31–46. God's passionate preferential option for the poor bookends Jesus' ministry and is powerfully enacted throughout the Gospels: "Just as you did it to one of the least of these who are members of my family, you did it to me" (Matthew 25:40). It is the first priority in the sense that the Gospels strongly suggest that if the Church does not engage directly in this ministry, then there is not much point in doing any of the rest—not a new message but one offered unhesitatingly by the Old Testament prophets. It's Teresa of Avila's great point: if prayer does not lead us to greater love and service, then it is either pointless or even bad for us.

Christian communities can do this ministry in all sorts of ways. Supporting projects such as food banks and street pastors are two obvious and widespread examples. But the point about direct delivery by the local Christian community is that it teaches us in practice what it means to be followers of Jesus. I am deeply impressed that a friend of mine who works nationally on homelessness policy also spends his Friday evenings as a volunteer in a soup kitchen—precisely so he cannot forget the link between what he is seeking to do at work and the real human need it is intended to address.

Kingdom values lead to kingdom living by kingdom people. And while sharing in common worship is necessary for Christians, it is not sufficient. It has to lead us out to serve, to the offering of our lives for others in love and compassion. There is an absolute, umbilical connection. That should not come as a surprise to us as it is written into the Gospels in Jesus' summary of the law: love God and love your neighbour as yourself (Mark 12:30–31). The clear connection with the Eucharist is beautifully captured in these words from a widely used prayer: "Through him we offer you our souls and bodies to be a living sacrifice; send us out in the power of your Spirit to live and work to your praise and glory."

At Derby Cathedral, where I used to serve, the nave becomes a night shelter once a week through winter. And if that means worshippers sometimes have to put up with surprising consequences, that's all part of the learning, part of what it means to be followers of Jesus in practice. In Harrogate, where I served as vicar after Derby, the neighbouring town-centre church was not known for the size of its congregations (though they were large), or the singing of their choir (though it was fantastic), or the beauty of their building (though it was stunning). The church was known for the fact that daily for twenty-five years the congregation had served breakfast to homeless people from across the town.

Chelmsford Cathedral—like most churches—is not a model of best or even good practice. Even our relationship with Colin had all sorts of ambiguities, and in the end his funeral didn't take place at the cathedral because of them. But our Wednesday afternoon drop-in and the active ministry of a small number of seriously committed lay people on the networks of addicts and the homeless is a genuine game changer. And I am delighted that much of this ministry takes place in the cathedral building itself—very visible in the north transept as others gather round the altar for the lunchtime Eucharist. During Choral Evensong last night one of our most challenging local heroin addicts walked gently down the nave, made herself a cup of coffee at the hospitality table, bowed slightly uncertainly, and went back out into the city centre. That's the kind of church I want to serve.

William Temple—one of the greatest Archbishops of Canterbury in modern history and the only one in the twentieth century to have been regarded as a genuine moral world leader—once said that the job of a Christian was to "seek grandeur where it is least expected and sorrow where it is thought to be hidden". That's a fantastic role description for every follower of Jesus—our "Magnificat mandate" where the values of the world are turned upside down by the values of the gospel; where we find that we are not measured by the splendour of our buildings or the glory of our worship, but by the quality of our love.

Servant leaders

My mother, Steve, appears regularly in "Dear Nicholas . . .". She was a very extraordinary person; noisy, loving, angry. From a complex and privileged Yorkshire Catholic Recusant background, she found herself married to an Anglican vicar in a dying mill town in east Manchester. Deeply devout and endlessly expressive she both loved the Church and—like many—found herself in a critical engagement with it.

Among her inexhaustible supply of challenging stories, she had a favourite for those occasions when senior clergy were gathered round our dining table. It was an incident on Leeds station. Mum was waiting for a train back to Liverpool with a crowd of Anglican, Roman Catholic and Free Church clergy. It was the end of a great ecumenical gathering with a buzz of conversation and multiple farewells.

She noticed a rough sleeper approach the gathering hopefully. He began begging for food, money, whatever he could get. Mum was fascinated and then appalled that no one seemed to notice. At last one of the senior clergy detached himself from the group, bought the rough sleeper a sandwich, and—having bought himself one too—sat down on the platform to talk with him as they ate.

The story passed into family folklore as mum used it again and again to invite Church leaders to think seriously about the kind of example they need to give, the kind of Christ they seek to follow, and the kind of servant leaders they should be.

This is a huge challenge, and the Church needs to listen—not to my mother so much as to the clear teaching of Jesus in the scriptures, because our traditions about leadership and hierarchy have become seriously messed up.

I was really shocked some years ago, when I was acting archdeacon for a year through a time of major pastoral reorganization. I am sufficiently self-aware to know that "promotion" in the Church is an upside-down affair. A member of our congregation used to work in Northern Uganda where the local bishop reminded himself every day that "every step up is always a step down!" That captures well what leadership might be like in response to Jesus' comment: "It is not so among you!"

But as my diary filled up with apparently important meetings, strategic engagements, and new responsibilities for parish appointments and the pastoral care of some seventy clergy and 180 congregations, I was shocked by how impressed I became with myself. In subtle ways, I realized that people behaved slightly differently towards me. One of my assistant priests told me that I definitely needed to dress better. And I actually bought a new jacket.

It is extraordinary that we should have constructed Christian ministry in this way. Our foundation documents tell a different story. It is hugely significant that in place of a welter of possible grand alternatives, the apostolic Church chose three quite unremarkable words for ordained elders: servant, elder and overseer (deacon, presbyter and bishop). In their day these really were completely ordinary words—you could have a bishop of a building site as much as of a church or kitchen. Presbyter really does just mean "old man". And servants were almost literally two a penny. Gloriously— as Ignatius of Antioch notes—the *deacon* is the one who represents Christ, precisely because ministry is all about service, all about love in action for a world in need.

The New Testament and the Christian tradition never use the word "leader" of a Christian minister. It is a word that only emerges in the mid- to late-twentieth century in this context. You can see why. We are embarrassed by many of the traditional words (and I know that my use of the phrase "ordained elder" mostly just annoys people). And, of course, all the organizations we want to look like have leaders. But—as Jesus says explicitly—"It is not so among you!" If you look at that passage carefully (Matthew 20:20–28; Mark 10:35–45; Luke 22:24–27), you'll see that Jesus uses a whole range of words for leadership, power and authority, and then explicitly and emphatically rejects them as titles for ordained elders in the Christian community.

Christians have found it extremely easy to forget all this. Words for the consecration of the ministry of ordained elders swiftly shifted ground from the simple, fairly colourless New Testament phrase "laying on of hands" (*cheirotonesis*) to the secular Latin word *ordinatio*, the word for installing a magistrate. Gradually different grades of ordained elders adopted splendidly hierarchical robes—power dressing with a range of elaborate headgear, despite Jesus' absolute clarity about the need for the Church to subvert precisely such power. Every time I put on the traditional vestments for the Eucharist, I am profoundly conscious that these are not the distinctive robes of a Christian priest, but the borrowed robes of a fourth-century Roman official. That does not necessarily mean they should not be worn. Rather that the wearer and the worshipping community should understand the irony. "It is not so among you!"

But it is in inward rather than outward ways that the Christian community needs to rediscover or reconfigure its ordained elders as servant leaders. This is precisely what Christians of all traditions have begun to see in Pope Francis—not in externals but in the manner in which he inhabits his office and the emblematic choices he makes.

Jesus himself could not be clearer: he gives Simon the intentionally ironic name "rock", because he is constantly getting things wrong—from the transfiguration to Gethsemane to the cross. Jesus teaches us that in his new Israel there are no hierarchies except those upside-down beatitude "hierarchies" of holiness, where the first are last and the greatest is a servant (or sitting with a beggar on Leeds station).

How can Christian communities today begin to respond? There are some clear invitations. Once again we are a minority across Europe. Old alliances with power are either broken or seriously creaking. Those who have shared the extraordinary privilege of long years in inner-city communities know very well that no one pays us any attention at all, unless we earn our right to be there. The church of today—like all voluntary sector organizations—earns its place at the table not through assuming that traditional privileges are still in place but by lives of servant leadership. And in my experience that is easily as true in leafy suburbia as in the inner city, just less obvious because people are more polite.

The ministry of the Church—certainly ministry in the Church of England—is always facing outwards, serving and present in the networks of the wider community; instinctively world/community facing rather than church facing. That's not just about membership of school governing bodies and running food banks but holding multiple overlapping networks across the community which it is the local church's job to serve.

I've spent fourteen years out of thirty-two serving in poor urban communities where this purpose is absolutely clear. The church spends itself in service of its community. That's the church's job. Crucially the service offered is not instrumental. It is for its own sake, not to achieve another good (though there may be other legitimate outcomes). It is our response to the good news of Jesus Christ who preaches the kingdom and comes to serve, not to be served. The great phrase, "Jesus preached the kingdom, but along came the Church", attributed to the nineteenth-century French priest and philosopher Hugues Felicité Robert de Lamennais, should be sobering and challenging for us and indeed for all Christians in post-Christendom Europe. That is especially true given how easy it is in times of challenge and change for the Church and its ministry to look inwards, to be preoccupied with itself as the focus of ministry rather than as the place from which we are sent.

One of the most challenging issues—and one that constantly saps energy and vision—is the extent to which we have turned our backs on this core kingdom orientation and instead poured our energies into simply running an organization. Our rhetoric, preaching and policies often remain kingdom oriented and outward facing, but where we put our energies and best resources does not. We have ignored the Weberian truism that the more organized an organization becomes, the further it moves from the people it is there to serve.

One of the most pernicious tendencies of the last forty to fifty years across the churches has been the vast numbers of clergy, unclear about what they were there for anymore, who have chosen to become chaplains to congregations rather than vicars for communities—becoming sheepdogs instead of shepherds. It is a very effective, organizational way of keeping busy, but it completely undermines the mission of the Church. Many clergy use the word "parish" to mean congregation rather than wider community, and modern developments in pastoral care often suggest that it is simply a series of soft disciplines practised largely in relation to the worshipping community. If the Church is training and deploying ordained elders simply to provide ecclesiastical events for people who enjoy that kind of thing, rather than to train people to be citizens of the kingdom, it has completely lost its purpose.

I'm really clear that my ministry as a priest has always been outward facing. I was never called to run a church, and—with the odd lapse—I never have. And that's what I see in dad's ministry. When he worked for twenty years with Bishop David Sheppard, dad used to say that they made a great team because of their complementary character and gifts—David bouncing off the world and dad bouncing off the Church. But dad's ministry—as priest and bishop—was deeply immersed in the world precisely as the arena of God's action, as the place where we live our lives and above all as the place to which we are sent as followers of Jesus. Yes, dad deeply committed to sustaining and developing the Christian community—but always as a dynamic, outward-facing movement rather than an institutional structure.

Don't get me wrong. There are inevitably elements of church management that go with the territory of being an ordained elder. But if that becomes the primary role (or even just a bit bigger than it should be), again, we've lost the mission before we've begun. The additional tragedy here is that with far more lay people now involved in active ministerial tasks, we have frequently constructed their role as inward facing, further embedding the idea that ministry is about the church.

The challenge of our contemporary context—and a theme that runs through "Dear Nicholas . . . "—is the renewal of the Church's self-understanding as kingdom people. Robert Warren—the former Church of England national officer for evangelism and the author of *Building Missionary Congregations*—notably referred to "the Church of England—a minority community with a majority complex". This and related pathologies still influence decision making at all sorts of levels in the Church of England.

We need to learn—now as a minority community yet with an extraordinary mission—to use our resources to go where Jesus goes and do what Jesus does. God isn't going to bless a Church that has abandoned inner-city communities, and he isn't going to bless churches that fail to deliver transformational social programmes. Indeed, the only things I'm really proud of during my time as Dean of Chelmsford are two things I had nothing to do with except saying "yes": the hospitality we provide day by day for rough sleepers, and the English for Women project which gives access to more than seventy women for basic English tuition three times a week.

Crucial to the renewal of our self-understanding is the rediscovery that we are not here to service an institution and that vicars (and indeed ministers of all sorts) are not here to run churches. Rather we are here as agents of community transformation for the sake of the kingdom (again Luke 4 and Matthew 25).

And again, none of this is instrumental. We don't do this to achieve another good than the good it is in itself. We spend ourselves in the service of others, kneeling to wash servants' feet before they feast. We do that because that's what our calling and purpose is. Our obsession with our own importance—which now looks extraordinarily threadbare—undermines our best intentions again and again. Inevitably it embeds an anxiety which leads us to use our resources primarily for preservation rather than for outward-facing ministry. It is often the marginal ministries, like that of a priest who goes to live on a housing estate with her family but no church building or community to see what happens, that recall the Church to its primary mission—working to develop networks and partnerships, and planting worshipping communities to serve those community networks.

I want to finish with a great quote. It's not as catchy as many I've used, but it struck me forcibly when I first read it. I was a few years into a decade living and working in a hugely deprived community in west Newcastle. And we'd just had three children in seventeen months. In so many ways I had no idea what I was doing. On a short, much-needed holiday in Oban, I found myself picking up a copy of the *Glasgow Herald* and reading these fantastic words by Ron Ferguson, then leader of the Iona Community. Ever since it's had the power to remind me of what the point of all this is:

> The Church, for all its manifest sins, is the broken-backed bearer of a story with transformative power at its heart. Now that's what's really important.

A "converting ordinance": The Eucharist as a missionary service

You and I would both share John Wesley's view that Holy Communion is a "converting ordinance". You and I, like him, have always seen the Eucharist as one of the great missionary opportunities for the Church. I'm very aware that in England today that would be a very minority view! Alison White, now Bishop of Hull, used to say that the problem wasn't the Eucharist that was the barrier but the way we celebrate it. And here, in my final short offering, I want to continue a conversation you and I started when I was a teenager.

> And as [Jesus sat] at dinner in the house, many tax-collectors and sinners came and were sitting with him and his disciples. When the Pharisees saw this, they said to his disciples, "Why does your teacher eat with tax-collectors and sinners?" But when he heard this, he said, "Those who are well have no need of a physician, but those who are sick. Go and learn what this means, 'I desire mercy, not sacrifice.' For I have come to call not the righteous but sinners."
>
> *Matthew 9:10–13*

There was a priest-tramp in London in the 1920s. It was not a ministry he had chosen, but one that had chosen him: as his life fell apart, with no nets to catch him, a late-Edwardian cleric found himself not working *for* or *alongside* the poor. No: he found himself poor, another inhabitant of the invisible cardboard city.

And living as he did—priest and pauper—he wrote a letter to the bishop asking for a licence to celebrate Holy Communion; to celebrate Holy Communion there on the streets of London, again, not as a priest *for* or *alongside* the poor, but as priest broken and poor himself. The bishop was inevitably unable to say yes. But I suspect the Eucharist was celebrated nonetheless by that priest, and the body blest and broken that the broken might be whole.

Eucharist, Holy Communion, Mass: Christian tradition uses many words for this—for this celebration of Christ's presence in bread and wine in obedience to his command. In our family traditions they have mingled freely: Holy Communion, that quintessentially Anglican word speaking of the four ways of communion (with God, with one another, with Christians across cultures today and with the Church down the centuries). Eucharist—a beautiful word: thanksgiving. But also a very useful word in the post-denominational context in which I have served my whole ministry, a word without a history, not owned by any one tradition. And then Mass—the word used by Scandinavian Lutherans and Roman Catholics, and also (as you know) the word we grew up with.

In childhood I used to think Mass meant something deeply mysterious—I remember being boat boy on Maundy Thursday with clouds of incense and vast numbers of candles on the altar. It came as a surprise later when I learnt Latin at school to discover that the word Mass actually means "*get out of here*!" Extraordinary! The same word as *mission*.

We have made Eucharist in an extraordinary range of places. In a converted shop in Byker, east Newcastle; in the glorious basilica at Vézelay with the monks and nuns of the Community of Jerusalem; by a distant river on a wet and windy Palm Sunday; high in the Ethiopian highlands; in the Mohave desert; with a tiny community of Armenians left behind in an east African city; with a small community of monks in western Crete on Easter Day (which you will remember was my eighteenth birthday!) This cosmic action made local; these local communities connected through this sacrament across cultures and history.

The Eucharist a "converting ordinance"? The problem is not with the Eucharist but with the way we celebrate it. We have taken Eucharist and imprisoned it in church—not just in buildings, but in grand ecclesiastical categories and definitions; in warring theological principles, and in traditions that often owe little to Scripture and Christian history and a great deal to our own unquestioned, unreflexive ideologies. Bound round with rules and definitions, church decides to own Eucharist rather than receive it as gift.

Many years ago, at a Mass in the local Roman Catholic Church for the Week of Prayer for Christian Unity, the priest of course gave Communion to everyone present—Anglicans, Methodists, Roman Catholics, even the odd independent evangelical. As a result, a scandalized parishioner wrote straight to the bishop to complain about this breach of the rules.

Like my Edwardian priest-tramp, it's the kind of mini-tragedy that points towards the heart of the problem: how has the bread of life and the cup of salvation, how has the place of cosmic encounter, how has the place of transformation become instead the dry re-enactment of apparently private rituals by "those who understand"?

John Wesley's point that the Eucharist is a "converting ordinance" drives something of a coach and horses through this. This is the key evangelistic service, and in early days Methodists even timed their meetings for worship so that people could still go to the Eucharist at the Anglican parish church, at least at Christmas and Easter. In many churches today, it would be hard to see how on earth the Eucharist could be a "converting ordinance", perhaps above all because we have gradually transformed it into a meal for insiders, rather than a sacrament of God's kingdom for the world. Again, not the Eucharist as a barrier to evangelization, but the way in which we celebrate it.

The Eucharist lies at the centre of my own Christian life. I grew up in a community where the daily celebration of the Eucharist was normal alongside the celebration of Morning and Evening Prayer. And that's the pattern written into the daily life of a cathedral. My experience in all sorts of different communities has been a huge variety of distinctive patterns of celebration which capture a vision beyond words or definitions and through which the Eucharist speaks in fresh ways—but only as long as we look intentionally at what lies beyond our doors, and those who may be hovering outside seeking a way through, a way forward, a way to cross the threshold. One of the great features of Derby Cathedral are the great glass doors at the west end. Whether on a Sunday or a weekday, when you stand at the altar you cannot avoid looking straight out into the street.

The history of the Eucharist has been one of people building walls. In the pages of the New Testament itself we find traces of the endless debate about whether children should be baptized and therefore whether they should be admitted to the Eucharist.

But also in the New Testament—as in the Gospel passage I began with—we have those powerful images of Jesus holding parties with tax collectors and sinners; of Jesus telling us that the kingdom is like a wedding banquet where the rich and powerful are no longer invited, only the poor and the outcast—those who can be dragged in from the highways and byways and from under the hedgerows. A whole—sometimes forgotten—history that speaks of the Eucharist not so much as a select gathering in an upper room but as the place where Jesus has fellowship with us in all our brokenness and need; the Eucharist as the place where the poor and the broken are the first guests at the table.

Maybe organized—and organizing—Christianity needed more rules. Great superstructures and hierarchies that gradually turned the Eucharist from meal and sacrament into performance and spectacle. By the thirteenth century, the people of God were routinely not allowed to receive the wine of the Eucharist; a couple of hundred years later the bread followed suit. In the high middle ages—as in some of the Orthodox

Churches today—people received the Eucharist maybe twice in a lifetime.

The Reformers tried to change all this, of course. For the *Book of Common Prayer* weekly Communion is the expectation. But people were so unused to this that they couldn't make the leap. And church leaders started putting so much stress on whether people were worthy to receive the sacrament at all that it hardly encouraged mass participation (forgive the pun).

It may be significant that for the first 1,000 years—and still in the Eastern Churches today—Christians didn't start the Eucharist by saying sorry and how unworthy they were to be there. Penitence only creeps into the Latin Mass—and from there into the *Book of Common Prayer*—very late in the day. The undoubtedly beautiful Prayer of Humble Access may not always be the right response to the invitation of the Lord to the abundant feast of life ("We are not worthy so much as to gather up the crumbs under your table . . . " Yes we are! God in Christ has made us worthy!)

Let's remember that altar rails were put there to prevent dogs and other animals getting near the sacrament, not for people to kneel at. We come not as suppliants, or even dogs, for that matter; we come, "ransomed, healed, restored, forgiven" as guests invited to a feast.

We build physical barriers, spiritual barriers, emotional barriers and doctrinal barriers. History sometimes helps to turn upside down our expectations. So as the Church of England has for nearly fifty years been debating whether children should receive Communion, the great Augustine of Hippo, writing 1,500 years ago, tells the adults of his flock that they are to learn from children how to receive Communion.

When I was a vicar in Harrogate, serving a congregation with many young families and with a significant children's ministry, children were welcome to receive the sacrament. One Sunday, a very young girl who I knew had already received Communion, came back and said, "Can I have one for my friend?" What a fantastic moment! She knew she had received a gift, and she had understood that this was a gift for sharing. Again, words from Augustine of Hippo: "*You* are to be taken, blessed, broken and distributed that the work of the incarnation may go forward."

This is a startling and wonderful opening-up of what it could mean to respond to Jesus' command "Do this in remembrance of me." The gospel constantly challenges us to break open our understanding of making Eucharist. In what way are we here responding to Christ's table-fellowship with the lost and the least? In what way are we celebrating realities of life-changing, world-changing priority here, rather than simply seeking our own comfort and refreshment? Or, worse still, just "making *my* Communion"?

Change may come through rewriting and reimagining our current confused policies on baptism, confirmation and first Communion. But it is much more likely to be through bold and scary experiment. When my last curate in Newcastle was ordained priest, she celebrated her first Mass with all the full ceremonial—extravagant robes, candles and incense. But the celebration took place on a piece of waste ground opposite the community centre near the bus stop, with a power cable from the chemist's next door feeding the sound system and the bouncy castle. There we were, surrounded by children, curious passers-by, visitors from more respectable parishes, our own congregation. It was the Eucharist of the Church; it was bread for the world, a world of hunger; it was wine for all people, people who thirst.

Robin Gamble, for many years a missionary priest in Bradford, used to drag an altar into the clubland area of that city, put on his robes and celebrate the Eucharist at 10 p.m. on Saturday nights. He still says it's the scariest thing he's done. But also that he learnt more about what the Eucharist could be than he ever imagined.

As "Dear Nicholas . . . " makes clear, in a not altogether approving way, I have spent more time with monks and hermits than would be typical. That's had a massive influence on my life and some of the marginal, prophetic figures from those traditions inspire me today. One of my lifelong heroes is Charles de Foucauld. After a colourful military career and various paths that didn't work out, he found himself living as a hermit in the Sahara. He said his prayers and sought to recommend the gospel to the neighbouring Moslem Touareg people. He celebrated the Eucharist with his Muslim server and had a curious but extraordinary practice of taking the bread consecrated at the Eucharist and burying it in the desert. It's a practice not covered by canon law, but it is a fantastic metaphor for the job of the Church in the twenty-first century—to plant Eucharist in the desert. Charles did not make a single convert in his lifetime, an offering of apparent failure. But today that part of the Sahara blossoms with his spiritual sons and daughters.

If there is a priest-tramp somewhere out there walking the cardboard city, my hunch is that the bishop would respond differently to the request to give him a licence to function as a priest. And maybe, across barriers of culture and expectation, we could have a conversation that leads all of us into a bigger room together. "Why does your teacher eat with tax-collectors and sinners?" Because that is what he does. We go where Jesus goes, and we do what Jesus does.

"Do this in remembrance of me." Was ever such a command so obeyed? Well, yes and no. This cosmic feast; this simple supper; this gorgeous ceremony; this wedding party. This "sacred feast, in which Christ is received, and the memory of his passion is renewed: our minds are filled with grace and a pledge of future glory is given us". This sacrament where Christ is encountered; this sacrament where Christ feeds us; this sacrament where Christ bleeds for his world. This meal at which the naked are clothed, the hungry are fed and the poor hear good news.

The celebration of the Eucharist is indeed a converting ordinance, and the Church of the third millennium will need to find its own way to rediscover this. The Eucharist is gospel-shaped and speaks of nothing other than God's self-emptying love, and God's invitation to us to become ourselves a sacrament of God's kingdom for the world.

I want to finish with some words by Father John Medcalf, a Roman Catholic priest who worked for many years in Latin America. It's doggerel rather than poetry, but it captures for me the missionary imperatives we face, and which the Eucharist has unique power to answer:

> I dream of a church where love and people
> are more important than stone and steeple.
> I dream of a church with an open door,
> where no one is privileged except the poor.
> I dream of a church where milk and honey
> will flow more freely than power and money.
> I dream of a church where young and old
> will be inspired to change their world.

Lightning Source UK Ltd.
Milton Keynes UK
UKHW051515160420
361796UK00006B/247

9 781789 590647